DARK ROADS AND STRANGERS

A HEART'S JOURNEY THROUGH PAIN

By

Michele Spaccarotella

ISBN: 1-4033-9916-6 (e-book)
ISBN: 1-4033-9917-4 (Paperback)

Library of Congress Control Number: 2002116311

This book is printed on acid free paper.

Printed in the United States of America
Bloomington, IN

1stBooks – rev. 02/26/03

IN MEMORY OF
Joseph J. Spaccarotella

On December 13, 2002, a very special man went home. That man was my father, Joseph Spaccarotella.

He was a man of gentle strength, a man of compassion and love, patience and wisdom. He was a simple and humble man whom everyone loved, none more than me. He taught me to be like him.

He never knew about this book because it was to be a surprise. Maybe it is better that way, for as a father, the pain that I suffered would have hurt him tremendously. In my heart I know that he knows about this now and maybe it doesn't hurt as much. And I know that he is very proud of me. I love you Dad.

Silent screams echo loudly;
The heart is torn in two…
Its blood spills forth to nowhere.

DEDICATION

This is dedicated to a man who shall remain anonymous. His name is not important. He knows and I know and that is all that matters. What is important is that he was the inspiration to write because he was the inspiration to feel. Without him and without what passed between us, none of this would have come to be.

He was gift and I treasure the time I had with him. He brought me great joy and because of that joy, brought great pain as well. I do not regret one minute of it.

Maybe someday our paths will cross again.

Thank you for all you gave to me, for all you were for me. I was privileged to have that time with you.

May God bless you.

ACKNOWLEDGMENTS

This book is the result of several people believing that I had something to say and that others needed to hear it.

A special thank you to my friend Carmela. Without you and your faith in me, I never would have done this. You were the first one to hear what I had written. You encouraged me from the very beginning and always believed in me, even when I didn't believe in myself. You listened endlessly. You cried with me and you laughed with me. Your friendship has been a gift.

Thank you to Donna for your help with the illustrations. You understood my pain.

Thank you to my brother Michael and my sister-in-law Cheryl for allowing me use of their computer and for my intrusion into their home and their time, and a special thank you to Cheryl for your last minute help. Your help and support has been greatly appreciated.

Lastly, thank you to Carol, Crystal and everyone who offered an encouraging word and buoyed me up when I began to doubt myself. You know who you are.

Above all, thank you to my God who brought me through all the things I needed to go through to make me the woman I am today and for always being there to lead me and carry me if need be.

Thank you all and may God bless each and every one of you.

Once Upon A Time...

Once upon a time there was a little girl who dreamed of someday loving someone. She dreamed of becoming a young woman and falling in love and having someone fall in love with her. She dreamed of growing old together and living happily ever after.

The little girl grew up but her dream never changed. Her friends all wanted to grow up to be somebody, to do great things, and to have many things, but deep inside she wanted only to love and to be loved and to give that to someone who she could spend the rest of her life with. Nothing else was as important as being able to love.

As she grew up, her heart remained innocent and trusting and maybe somewhat naïve because she believed everyone felt the same. They didn't. And her heart was hurt. But she continued to trust and to believe.

One day it seemed as if the dream had come true and for many years she was able to give that love. Soon there were even little ones to be loved. She poured everything she had into all of them, her whole being was for them and because of that she became all she was meant to be…a vessel of love.

She found out though that happily ever after doesn't exist. She wasn't naïve to the fact that life has its ups and downs. She was realistic enough to know this and she believed that the good comes with the bad, but together it can be conquered.

It wasn't true, for the bad came and then the bad became worse until her heart, her soul, her spirit were crushed. She believed they were so crushed they would never be whole again. And she wondered if there was anybody that sought out the simplicity of love, not the false illusions of what we are told we should want, but just the simpleness of love.

She decided she wouldn't seek this ever again. It was too painful. She would care about others, but she wouldn't let them get close enough to touch or to see where she kept her heart hidden. There were times she yearned to let her heart out, but she always resisted because the pain of resistance is far less than the pain of betrayal and rejection.

But one day something happened and she became frightened and confused because someone was entering into that place. She became terrified, so afraid of feeling that pain again and she didn't know what to do. So she tried to keep the door closed and she tried to hide her heart even deeper, but it was no use because there was such gentleness and tenderness and those eyes, those eyes that held hers. And she let him in. She felt so safe, so cared for and she began to think it wasn't so bad after all. Even if it couldn't be, he would tell her gently and with compassion.

He didn't. He told her it was a lie and that gentle heart that only sought to love and to be loved was betrayed once more. She was wrong too because he never told her why and he didn't tell her with gentleness and compassion. He was harsh and cold and she broke once more.

So now she picks up the pieces and wonders where she will hide them and wonders about happily ever after and if anyone seeks hearts of simpleness and love anymore. And then she decides she will not seek this ever again because her trust and her spirit have been taken away.

This is the story of that little girl who wanted only to love and to be loved. It is her story, her heart's journey through pain, of dark roads and strangers.

The Journey...

I do not consider myself a writer, but rather just an ordinary person trying to get through this thing called life. Life bombards us with many painful experiences. Some of us experience more pain than others, but none of us can escape it.

Pain is difficult to articulate. How does one describe it? How do you describe the feeling of heartache, the gripping, shattering interior pain of the heart? Interior pain is difficult to explain and even more difficult to alleviate. It shatters, it kills, hearts are broken, relationships are severed, hopes are lost. We've all been there, we've all experienced it or will experience it.

What I've written in the pages that follow are my experiences with this heartache. It is my personal journey through the pain of cancer and heartache, of a heart broken and hopes shattered. These words were not intended for others to read. They were written for me in my time of pain, when I was at my lowest and I found that trying to write my emotions was helpful. I never intended to write a book and it was not an easy decision for me to make. By writing this, I expose myself and leave myself vulnerable for perhaps even more pain. I was encouraged by friends who believed that others might benefit from my pain and something deep within kept urging me to do this as well. Putting those emotions into words can be so difficult to do and I was encouraged to share what others also feel, but cannot say. It is with some degree of fear that I take this step but one which calls me to trust that there is a higher purpose to all of this.

I suffered the pain of divorce after twenty-five years of marriage. Divorce is never easy, but this became rife with abuse; emotional, psychological and physical. The scars run very deep. I spent twenty-seven years of my life in a relationship and when it was all over, I came to realize that those years were eating away at me, at the person I was inside, at my self-esteem, and my self worth as a person and as a woman.

I spent five years of very conscious efforts trying to heal the wounds that had been inflicted on me. I was involved in many forms of healing. Many years were spent in therapy. I attended healing classes and seminars, spiritual retreats and prayer sessions. I continue to meet regularly with a spiritual director. I needed healing on many levels; emotional, psychological, physical and spiritual. It is not an easy road and it is not a quick road to healing. I had lost so much…a way of life, a home, friends. I was estranged from my children. I didn't know who I was or even if I was worth anything. I had been told so many things about myself that I began to believe the lies.

Over time, the efforts I had made to heal were starting to show results and I was starting to feel as if I was moving in the right direction. I was beginning to feel good about myself. It was then that I was diagnosed with breast cancer and my world was once again torn apart. I was thrown into turmoil, especially now being alone.

The months that followed were terrifying and not something anyone wants to go through. I know well the effects of cancer and the treatment of it on the body as well as on the emotions. Surgery was followed by five months of chemotherapy and then six weeks of daily radiation treatments. I know the effects of the drugs, what they can do physically and mentally. I felt the sickness, the depression, the loneliness as well as the fear. And during this walk through hell, I also felt the pain of heartache once again. My body and my mind became worn out. The drugs and their side effects took their toll. With breast cancer, physical appearance changes and baldness becomes a way of life. As a woman with this disease, I lost two very distinct parts of what makes me a woman, breasts and my hair. I felt cheated and so very unattractive. All of this now added to the feelings and the wounds that were already a part of my life.

However, what had been taking place in my spiritual healing over these years led me to now believe so strongly that there was a purpose for me with this cancer and I believed this even before the final diagnosis was confirmed. From deep within me, I knew it was cancer even before the doctor told me those chilling words, but I believed that God had a reason. I knew that He would use me for His purpose and for His glory and that He would take care of me. He did just that. I still did not want to travel this road and it was still very difficult, but knowing what I did helped me.

As I look back on my life, I realize how close God has always been to me and how natural my relationship with Him has always been. He has been as close to me as the air that I breathe and just as essential to my life. Each breath has been Him and without either one, life ceases. There was no reason to doubt that He would be there now for me.

Over the past years, He has brought me even closer to His heart and my relationship with Him has grown stronger. He has revealed Himself to me in so many ways. He has taken me into deeper water and called me forth out of the boat of safety to walk with Him. I haven't always wanted to go. Water terrifies me and I've found that sometimes He takes us to places we would rather not go. This journey with cancer was another call to follow. It isn't always easy to follow and I'm no different than anyone else. I want to do it my way because I think I know best and I don't always go willingly. But He has blessed me when I put my trust in Him. I believe my faith to be quite strong and yet I found this to be a very difficult road to travel.

The road of life is not an easy one. We struggle because we are human and our humanness is often weak. We hurt and we bleed. We don't want to suffer. Suffering is contrary to our human condition. It is something we run from, not willingly embrace. Sometimes we lose hope and want to give up and give in. I experienced all of these feelings. I hurt, I bled, I cried, and many times I asked how much more. Having a strong faith does not make one immune from life's hurts and life's tragedies. Often times we may feel it tests us even more.

My faith teaches that we are made in the image and likeness of God, having both human and divine elements, more human than divine since that divine element hasn't been perfected yet. Life helps us to perfect that as we travel the road before us and hopefully not making too many mistakes, hopefully always trying to follow His ways. But even those wayward paths help us if we are open to see the error of our ways. We will achieve that divine perfection someday, when we see Him face to face.

In those moments of great pain and suffering are also to be found great blessings if we are open to receive them. They are all around but one must be receptive to them and see with the eyes of faith. We will then see God in the middle of this and we are never alone, even though at times we may feel it.

My experience with cancer was very difficult and yet it was very easy for me, a paradox of sorts. How could it be easy and yet difficult? It was easy because God walked with me and God talked with me and He led me by the hand. I knew I was being cared for and I was able to see the abundance of blessings He bestowed on me. I was able to share and to minister to others in the middle of my storm.

It was also a most difficult time for me, because I was alone, relationships as they were and cancer is a difficult road to travel, even more difficult alone. I was afraid at times and I lost my way. I wanted to be held. I wanted someone I could lean on, a shoulder just for me. There were times I needed that human touch, someone there in the flesh, that shoulder, that hand, that touch. And I needed to feel that I was not damaged goods, because breast cancer does that to a woman.

It was during this time that I met someone who I thought would be that someone for me. It was frightening for me, after the betrayal and rejection of divorce. Facing cancer and facing the possibility of a relationship can be terrifying, yet somehow I felt safe and I allowed myself to trust. After all I had gone through, I never wanted to get close to anyone ever again but I found myself believing and trusting and opening up. This was different, or so I thought. I let the walls come down only to realize my worst fears had become reality. I heard words that I had hoped I would never hear.

I once again faced betrayal and rejection but this time I was staring death in the face. My heart screamed out in pain, it shouted in agony and I didn't see God in any of this and I didn't understand why He would allow this to happen. I didn't know how I would get through one day to the next. My faith told me He was there with me, but I didn't feel it and I had to make a very strong effort to believe that He was.

It was during this dark time that I picked up pen and paper, and trying to come to terms with all that was happening to me started to write what I was feeling. I wrote in the confusion and it was a means of trying to sort through my emotions. Most of the pain came not from the cancer, but what happened to me during the cancer. Had I just been faced with dealing with the cancer, I would not have felt the anguish that I did and I doubt I would have ever written. It was because of the betrayal of my trust which caused me such heartache and led to such pain. My writing, I believe was a means of survival. It was a means to try to find answers and to make sense of what had occurred. Because of the cancer, I struggled to understand how someone could do something like this.

It was from those darkest moments, those moments of excruciating pain and deep anguish that I wrote the words that follow in this book. My self-esteem was already wounded and now my hope was taken away and my energy to go on was gone. My life seemed doomed to nothingness and all that had given it new meaning was stripped away and left me feeling naked once again. Sometimes the anguish paralyzed me and the pain never seemed to end. I wrote then as part of my struggle to survive, to survive the betrayal of trust and to survive drowning in the despair and pain and to survive the cancer. I wrote in those moments when I lost hope and saw no reason to go on. I wrote at my lowest moments, very real and human moments.

There were times I could cry no more and the words just spilled forth. Most times I was unaware of exactly what I was writing. There were sleepless nights, words rushing through my head, my heart in pain and sleep not found until I turned on the tape recorder and let the words spill forth. It wasn't until the next day, when played back that I was astonished to hear what had been given me. I truly believe that this was a gift and helped me to deal with the deep pain that I felt. Perhaps because it was gift, that is the reason behind this book. I've left the words exactly as I wrote them since they were not intended for publication but rather as a means of expressing my pain. To change them takes away from the intensity of the pain I felt as I wrote.

I was always brought out of those moments and was led to the next day. God's angels sometimes carried me when I couldn't carry myself. But the pain was always there. I wish I could say that it has gone away. It hasn't. Sometimes I believe the pain to be worse and time has not healed those wounds. Pain ignored does not go away. It grows stronger and goes deeper. I need to heal from this and it is taking a very long time to do. I was touched very deeply and my heart broken. There are many unknowns and the unknown can hurt more than the known. Forgiveness and reconciliation are needed but not easy when only one seeks this.

I am in the process of healing since to not heal is detrimental to my health. The pain is with me constantly. I still cry, I still hurt and I still fall. Then I get up and try to move forward, always aware that God is with me, but sometimes not understanding His ways.

As you read these pages, know that you are not alone, even when you feel it most. Know too that all of us, even those whose faith seems strong, feel that faith shattered at times and feel pain and suffering. Many times those feelings cannot be put into words. If someone can identify with what I wrote, even if one person can be helped in their pain, then I know that God has used me once again to help another and none of this has been in vain.

Some of the world's greatest treasures, literature, art, music to name a few, were born of great pain. So much suffering gave birth to something so very beautiful. A heart broken open can sometimes help another to heal. God uses broken vessels to heal the brokenness that surrounds us. It is only when we are truly broken and empty can we then be filled with the compassion to reach out to others. It is with that compassion that we can then bring healing, both to ourselves and to those we touch and we then become wounded healers.

It is my hope that someone reading these pages will go from the dark ugliness of their pain to the warmth and radiance of a new day because someone else has been there and gone through it and come out on the other side, not pain free, but able to accept it and to go on despite the pain. If that happens, then there was a purpose to this after all. God bless.

Michele Spaccarotella

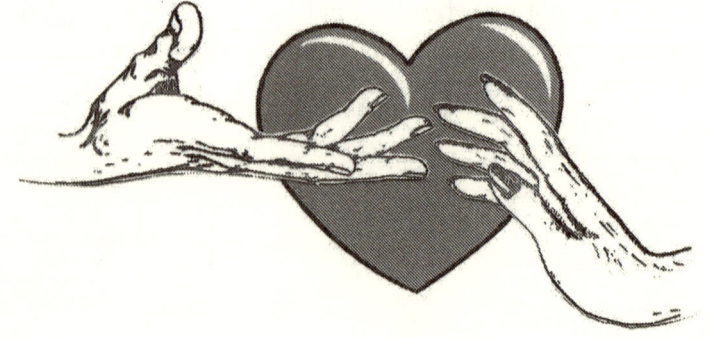

Hand touches hand and through it hearts speak.
You said without words as much or perhaps even
more than you said with words.

Hearts spoke when hands touched.

The Heart Exposed...

LONG AGO

Long, so long ago it seems I picked up the pieces of a broken life, a broken woman, a broken heart. The pieces of this broken life and broken woman were slowly put back together. But the heart is a different story.

Try as I might all the pieces would not go back, many being held by very loose threads with numerous cracks and fault lines that run very, very deep. And so because of this, I took this fragile heart, a heart that has so much love to give and put it away inside a very small box, carefully placing it inside lest a piece fall off and be lost.

I closed the lid and locked this little box behind a door into which no one could enter, for you see I threw away the key. Somehow, some way the key was found and the door unlocked.

With tender, caring hands that box was opened and gently, ever so gently, my wounded heart was touched. I let this happen. I let you in.

You hold my heart in your hands. Please hold it gently, for it is oh, so fragile. Look closely and you will see the tears it continues to cry. Please treat it tenderly for it has so much love to give.

23

But now I fear I must take back my heart for I was clearly mistaken. The heart that was broken has now been wounded again, the cracks opened wide. I must take it back, I must protect it again from the hands that I thought held it tenderly. I will lock it safely away once more where only I can peer within and remember the memory of what I thought was. This time I will destroy the key so no one can ever find it again for the pain is too great and my heart is too fragile to be touched like that again.

So I will place my heart into that little box once more and I will put a piece of you along side it, as a remembrance of something and someone who touched me, remembering everything but the pain. I lock this door with sadness for my heart was filled with so much hope.

Good-bye dear heart, you're safe now. No one can hurt you again. The door is locked, the key destroyed. Rest now and remember only the good things.

CANCER

Having cancer is such a difficult journey. You feel betrayed by your body, the body you've tried to take care of the best you can. And now it has betrayed you. Or is it that you have betrayed it? Maybe that's it, maybe you did something to cause this to happen. Maybe you could have prevented these killer cells from invading and you wonder how much they have already destroyed.

As a woman, you feel undesirable now. The cutting of the surgeon's knife has left you damaged. You are now disfigured, incomplete, less whole. Cancer does that to you. The poison that courses through your body now starts to do its work. It starts to kill and you feel this death within you. One day you look in the mirror and you don't recognize the person looking back at you because all you see is the death of who you once were. You are told not to worry, that the drugs are doing their job but you feel what has been killed within you and you can see that result with your eyes.

You look to those around you to hold you up, to carry you through this, but no one is there. It is then that you realize you must do this alone and the loneliness closes in and suffocates you as you take your first steps on this dark and unknown path.

You hear words somewhere in this darkness, somewhere in the distance. They become louder and stronger and you go towards them. "I want to understand," they say to you. "I will be there for you," and out of the darkness comes a hand…reaching, touching, holding. You come to realize that within that hand is your own hand and it feels so good, so right, so comforting and everything changes.

The path is not dark anymore. Now there is light, there is hope. The cancer has lost its sting and the strong medicine doesn't kill, it gives new life. All this because a hand reached out, because a heart spoke words, because someone touched another. New life sprang forth.

It didn't last. The light, the life, the hope, all snuffed out with just a few words. And from the darkness again comes a voice, but it brings no hope. "Not true," the voice says, "I didn't mean any of it." Not only has the body been betrayed, but now the heart as well, and it cracks and breaks as tears silently fall.

The path becomes black once more and the loneliness creeps in, rolls in like the fog enveloping all, obscuring everything. The path cannot be seen anymore and you struggle to find your way. You are alone again, alone with your betrayals and your cancer and you don't know why.

In the silence you listen and you wait, hoping to hear that voice once more, hoping to feel that hand reach out. It doesn't come, but still you wait.

THE DANCE

Do you remember when you asked me to dance, how your eyes met mine and you took my hand in yours?

You held my hands in yours, your body close to mine. You felt it. Your eyes said it all. Closer still you came. Your face gave it all away...your smile, your eyes, seeing into my heart.

You led this dance. I accepted.

The touch of your finger on my skin, whisper soft, a hint in your eyes, a smile on your face. I stirred deep within. You noticed. Your smile said you did.

Concern over tears shed. "Is it me?" you ask, holding my hands in yours, standing so very close, our bodies touching. Encouraging words, words of promise and hope. Yes, there could be hope, I thought.

All the while you were leading this dance. I held your hand and I followed you. Your words were the music.

But what is this? Not true, you tell me. Empty words...not really meant. "How can this be?" I cry out. I felt your touch, I looked into your eyes, I felt your closeness, I danced with you. "How could it not be?"

Michele Spaccarotella

You say the dance is over. You will not lead me again. I stand alone now, the pain washes over me, floods me deep inside. The dance floor is empty except for me. The music has ended. You are gone.

STRIPPED, NAKED, EXPOSED

My body has been betrayed by this disease. The poison runs through me, killing good and bad alike. I feel stripped and naked of who I am, knowing that my self, my identity is within, yet not knowing the person without. It is devastating, painful. I am alone.

Naked and exposed I stand before you. You know my aloneness and you reach out to me. Words to comfort, words to believe and trust. Hands touching, holding, feeling…something. You search my eyes. We speak. Trying, wanting to understand you seek me out time and time again. Hesitant, fearing the hurt that may follow, I struggle with this. You continue to reach out to me, your eyes continue to seek me out. Cautiously, I relent.

Fear of the hurt slowly vanishes. I can begin to believe and trust you. I see no reason not to. This disease, this poison has lost its effect on me now. You have taken that away, for you have touched my soul, my heart. You have given me hope. The strangeness outside is replaced by a strength from within. I no longer feel stripped or naked. I feel whole. I feel strong. I feel desired.

You will walk this with me. You will give me strength to continue. You will hold my hand along the way. We will come to know each other. I feel good.

Michele Spaccarotella

Something is terribly wrong. I see your indifference, your lack of concern and gentleness. I've done something to make you change. What is it that I have done to make this happen? "Nothing," you say, "you have done nothing." You don't want to know me. There was no truth to it at all. And all over again I stand stripped, naked and exposed. Stripped by the very hands that reached out to me. Stripped by the voice that sought to comfort me. Like the poison that runs through my body killing, your words run straight to my heart. They have done their deed. They have hit their mark. They have poisoned and killed.

I stand alone…stripped, naked, and exposed.

The wounds of the heart do not heal;
they cry silent tears.
Tears which no one can see.

Listen…listen with your heart.
Do you hear them softly falling?

Hearts hear what no one else can hear.
Hearts hear the silent tears.

Fingertips touch fingertips…
gently…
quietly…
softly.

Heart whispers to heart.
Listen! Can you hear it?

SILENT SCREAMS

I hear your words through silent screams. I feel the razor sharp pains as you say what I didn't expect to hear. It wasn't true, you didn't mean what you said. And my heart, that heart which was foolishly opened to you now lays shattered, the pieces like shards of glass, brittle, needle fine, crushed underfoot.

How could this be? Why is this happening? I believed you.
I sweep up these pieces, gathering them all quickly. Attempts to put this heart back together are futile.

No more will this heart be whole, no more will it venture forth to trust or try to love again, for it was much to fragile to withstand this pain. The silent screams echo loudly. Where once a heart dwelled is now a gaping hole, an icy blackness.

You played with me, with my emotions and with my heart. You came close, your eyes met mine and my heart spoke to yours, believing your heart heard these silent words. You took my hand in yours and your eyes held me close. You saw my aloneness, my vulnerable heart and you touched it so very gently, giving it a hope it dared not to hope in. It was afraid, but your touch persisted, your eyes searched me and your words encouraged me. I relented to you.

But you were only playing, not meaning what you said or did. Again the pain cuts through me and I hear those hurtful words.

My heart screams again, "run, hide, please protect me." The pain is now consuming me, engulfing my entire being. Where can I hide so the memory of your touch won't find me? Where can I go to escape the pain of you? I need protection, my heart is being destroyed.

Close the door, I must close the door against this onslaught. Sweep the pieces in…hurry.

It is too late. Do not try to put this heart together. It is forever broken. The love and caring it had to give lies shattered now. Do not rush for there is nothing left to protect. This heart will never be whole again, will never love again. This heart is no more.

Michele Spaccarotella

ENDLESS

The days last forever, minutes seem like hours, hours like days, endless, ongoing. Only sleep evades this until the dawn arrives to start all over again.

The pain is as endless as the day, constant, throbbing pain. Time with nothing to look forward to, no one to hold my hand.

Questions fill my head, answers are nowhere to be found. Crying, the heart seeks to be hidden, never wanting to be hurt like this again, begging me to make the pain cease. "Why?" it sobs to me. "Why did he do this?"

I have no answer to comfort this wounded, innocent heart. I am at a loss as to how to stop the hurt. Sobs turn to gut wrenching screams. This pain, so real, consumes it. How do I make it stop?

My heart continues to cry. I fear for it, broken beyond repair…this heart, so trusting, so loving. I fear it has been broken for good.

I tried to put the pieces back together once before. Helpless, I watched as the tears poured forth, begging me to stop the pain. I couldn't, so I locked it away. I locked away this heart so it wouldn't be hurt like that ever again.

Yet it has. Tears continue to fall. "Why did you let me out? Why did you let him touch me? You let me break again. You let me hope in the midst of none. Please stop the pain. Hide me. Do not let me out again. Trusting, hoping, caring is too painful. I cannot survive anymore."

Is that what you do to hurting hearts,
hearts that are in pain
you give them hopes,
you give them dreams
and let them live again?

And then when this has happened,
when high to the heavens they fly;
that is when you tell them,
it was all just a lie.

So to the earth they plummet,
from their journey to the stars;
hopeless, hurt and dying,
love gone…never more.

I never should have trusted you;
I should have been more wary,
    of your touch…
    of your eyes…
    of your words.

But I let them penetrate the walls around my heart;
    because time and time again you sought me out and
    brought me close to you.
However brief it was, you brought me close to you.

I should have resisted more.
I should have kept the door locked.
But it felt so good, so right.
And when your hand held mine in yours,
    whatever fear of the pain I had…
    vanished.

Such gentleness in your touch,
    such warmth when your eyes held mine.
What did I have to fear?
No harm could come to me,
    for you were there.
Our time together so short, so fleeting
    and yet so much seemed spoken in so little time.

So I opened the door…
    yet sometimes I think perhaps it was you
    who opened it.
It was you…you who walked in on me
    before I had the chance to protest your entry.
You who boldly took those steps and
    then it was too late.

37

You had crossed over into my heart and
    with that my heart took on wings.
You lifted me high, my heart came alive.
You held me up…you were the wind beneath my wings.
And then you were no more.

Spiraling downward;
    no chance to stop…
    falling…faster…faster;
    crashing to the earth below;
    broken and dying.

I never should have trusted you…
    never let your touch move me the way it did…
    never let your eyes hold and caress.

No matter where I run to hide
    I cannot escape your memory.
But I wonder…
    do broken and dying hearts hold memories still
    or do these memories get broken too;
    do they slowly die or
    do they remain when hearts stop?

I never should have trusted you.

My heart is heavy and in pain once again. Why did I let this happen? Why did I let you touch me so? My wounded heart, closed tightly against the world slowly opened to your touch like the petals of a flower as the warm sunshine caresses it. Like the sunshine kisses open each petal, your gentle touch slowly, carefully opened the petals of my fragile, yet unhealed, wounded heart. You hold that flower, my heart, in your hands.

You gave me hope. Hope that perhaps this time would be different. I didn't want to hope, afraid of the pain that might follow. And now, as I sit here nursing my pain and wiping away the tears of a crying, hurting heart, I realize that this is no different than before.

In your hands, gentle hands that caressed, you now hold my crying heart. Do you see the tears? Do you care enough to wipe them for me and hold close to your heart this broken one? I fear not.

I feel the pain of my vulnerability once again, of letting you into my very closed and private place. I fear the pain of losing that which I so much desired and I fear the loneliness that I know will follow.

I believed the words you spoke to me, words that filled me with hope. I believed what your touch said. Your eyes spoke to my heart and my heart answered you. Did you hear it? Gentle touches, ever so lightly gladdened my heart. Hands touching held a sensuousness that delighted me, left me wanting more and yet fearing the pain that might follow.

I am uncertain now as to what will become of me. Perhaps I should pluck the flower of my heart before the petals die and fall. Perhaps I can preserve my heart in full bloom with the tenderness I imagined you gave to it and hold it forever where no one will ever hurt it again.

So once again I enter that closed and private place. I place the flower of my heart inside and bid it farewell. It is safe in here and my heart is sheltered. As I leave, this flower that is my heart sheds a tear, but I know it is safe now.

I close the door.

What was it that happened between us? Paths crossed for a reason, of that much I'm certain. I knew it when I met you.

The ease I felt at being near you was startling, and yet…not so;
confusing…yet comfortable.

God works in strange way, doesn't He?

But what was it that happened between us, because it was more than what I knew or what I felt. It was what you knew and what you felt also.

What made you become so bold, so confident in knowing just how I would respond? What did you know in your heart? Did you feel the same things I felt?

How did you know that when you reached for me, taking my hand in yours, I would willingly come to you? How did you know that? And why did you take that step?

When your eyes searched mine and held me close, how did you know I would let you into that place hidden within? And why did you enter? It was a very risky step.

Yet you knew, didn't you? You knew I would let you in. How did your heart know this?

When you gently stroked my skin, how did you know I wouldn't pull away, but would instead tremble beneath your touch? When you came close, your body touching mine, so close I could feel your breathing, how did you know I wouldn't push you away and run?

Why did you become so bold and how was this all so easy for you to do? If you, who was so confident, who took that step, knowing I would step out to meet you, if you knew this, if you took that risk, then why did you run and leave me here all alone?

From somewhere deep within
   deep within the darkness
   emerges a fragile, wounded heart.
Hesitant, fearful, yet wanting to trust.
Blinking against the brightness of hope,
   it dares to reach out;
   to open;
   to touch and be touched.

Gentleness surrounds it.
Fearful no more it throws open the cloak of darkness;
   the cloak that bound and hid all this time.

Sunshine and warmth envelope and hold it close.
Oh! How alive it became, this fragile heart.
How it eagerly sought your touch;
   your smile;
   your gentle way.
Until…
   the cloak of darkness sprung forth to hide
   it once again.

And with it vanished the sunshine;
   the warmth.
And the cold darkness overcame this heart once
   more.

Brittle from the cold;
   shattered pieces lie broken…
   its life is gone.

Sometimes the only words the heart understands
are those of a hand being held or
the look in one's eyes.

Do you know what your eyes told me
when first we met;
your gaze…reaching beneath the veil
to reveal the hidden?

Like the dew gently kissing the budded rose
your touch kissed my tightly closed heart.
And like the early morning sunshine upon it,
it glistened with the possibilities of a new day.

CONSUMING EMPTINESS

The emptiness consumes me, the blackness covers me.
There is a hole where once a heart dwelled, a heart made to love and to be loved.
But now there is just a hollowness for the heart is gone, broken, I think beyond repair.

I always thought once broken, a heart felt no more.
I was wrong. Those broken, shattered pieces pierce my very existence;
   a pain beyond pain…
   until screaming, I beg it to stop.
The pain is unbearable.

What remains then, when hearts cease and pain is gone?
A numbness, I suppose, an ache beyond anything ever experienced.
And what becomes of all those heart pieces? Do they just lie there, crumbled, shattered and splintered or do they disappear over time?
Do hearts broken like this ever get mended, are they ever whole again, are they ever loved?

I fear not.
Maybe it is safer that way, for if never mended they can never break again;
   and no one can be allowed to enter, for there is
   nothing to enter into.
How can one enter into nothingness?

Yes, I believe it is better that way.
It is safer too.
No more hurt and pain…
    no more rejection and betrayal…
    no more breaking.
Let the emptiness consume me then;
    let the blackness cover me.
I bid thee farewell, my sweet, once loving heart.
We shall not meet again.
Let the emptiness in.
A heart shall not dwell in this place evermore.

There comes a time when the pain becomes so great you don't want to fight it anymore, when the struggle to overcome, overwhelms.

It is then that you just want to let go and let the pain swallow you, letting it permeate all of you…floating like the outgoing tide…riding on the waves to distant shores.

Maybe if you just let go, it will hurt less. Maybe it's the struggle against the pain that makes it hurt more. Maybe when you let go and stop the fight, just maybe, the pain will go away, because then you will have become one with it and you won't know anything else.

But…maybe not.

LIES

There is no one to care, no one to hold my hand. My heart has been wounded again, wounds on top of wounds. Your words cut like a knife...stabbing, piercing words.

Lies...it was all lies.

My heart screams in pain. It lies naked and exposed. Icy fingers grip its very core, twisting, crumbling, tearing it apart. Silent screams echo within. How do I escape this? How can I stop this pain?

Lies...it was all lies.

You came close. You played with my heart. Why? Didn't you see the tears falling? Didn't you see the pain already there? I know you did. And still you ventured in, touching, coming closer, closer, until...you stopped. Like a moth to a flame you came close. Do you fear coming too close? Do you fear the fire of my heart? Do not be afraid, for it is a fire of love, of life, not a fire of destruction.

But you stopped, crushing this heart as you did. It's broken. Do you see how it has been broken again? The hands that gently touched have been the very hands that have destroyed. See the pieces. Look closely and you will see yourself for you were a part of this heart that you have broken. Are you willing to gather these slivers of what once was? Are you willing to gather these pieces in those once gentle hands? Or will you drop these pieces to be crushed underfoot, ground into nothingness. It is then that my heart will cease to exist.

I am afraid. You were my hope. The pain is once more. You can stop it if you wish. Are you strong enough to let your heart answer for you?

Michele Spaccarotella

WHY?

You played with me.
You came close and you played with me.
You knew what you were doing.
You knew that I was alone and that I believed you.
And yet you did it anyway.

Why?
Why did you do that to me?

You could see in my eyes that I trusted you.
You could hear in my words that I believed you.
And still you came close; still you encouraged me.
You saw in my eyes what I saw in yours.
You knew my pain; you knew my struggle.
You touched my hand and ended up holding my heart.
You knew that.
You continued.

Why?
Why did you do that to me?

You saw that I responded to all you said and did.
You continued to touch me.
Now you tell me you don't want to.
Now you say it wasn't true.

Again I hear your words.
I ask as my heart struggles with this pain.
I ask as my heart slowly breaks.

Why?
Why did you do that to me?

Michele Spaccarotella

FORGET

I want to forget…
   the day I was told I had cancer;
   the day I saw my body less than whole,
     damaged and cut;
   the day the chemo started,
     flooding me with deadly poisons.

I want to forget…
   the day my hair fell out,
     leaving me stripped and naked for all to see;
   the days of sickness alone,
     reaching for a hand that wasn't there.

I want to forget…
   the struggle to go on;
   and the loneliness through the hell I had to walk.

I want to forget it all.

And yet it is these very things that I most want to
   remember…
   for in all of this,
     pieces of you are woven through.
In all of this, your presence looms.
In all of this was the hope of you that carried me.

Can you fix broken hearts? Can your gentle hands put back the shattered pieces, the pieces that lay like shards of glass, sharp and brittle, waiting to split into tiny pieces at the merest touch? Only gentle, caring hands can touch these delicate pieces. Are they your hands? Are you willing to take that chance and see what may occur once this heart is healed? Will you take that chance and see the love waiting inside?

Sometimes in life the opportunity comes around to right the wrongs we've done. Sometimes that person comes along to take that chance with, one who will make sense of all the negatives in our life. What we do when that occurs makes all the difference in the world.

I struggle to survive the anguish of the heart. I will not open my heart to another again. I will not let another come close enough to touch me. Bruised and wounded I must bid my heart farewell and hide it away where it will not suffer again. Hidden from the world it will be safe. Hidden from the memory of you it will not shed tears.

But how will I hide the memory of you, the gentleness I thought you meant? How do I hide from the feeling of your hand in mine or the look in your eyes? Where does a heart go to escape memories? In its broken state all it can do is to cry tears as sadness engulfs it and swallows it up.

How many times can a heart be wounded, can a heart be broken before it ceases to exist? Can it ever be whole again or does it slowly fall apart only to become unrecognizable, never to be touched again. Hearts were made to love and to be loved, not to be wounded and broken.

It is time to hide it away. Into the deep, dark, bottomless abyss I will place what is left of my heart. Into this dark place I will put the memories of you. I will let the darkness, the nothingness surround them, devour them. Maybe then the pain will cease, the tears will not be shed, the heart will not be wounded again, for hearts deprived of love soon cease to exist.

VOICES

Voices from the past fill my head…
   worthless,
   no good,
   no one will care again.
They fill me, screaming loudly, devouring me.

Then you came into my life. Your voice told me otherwise. Your touch encouraged me, gave me hope. The voices were quieted. You seemed interested. You came close. You held my hand. You ended up holding my heart. Now the voice of hope filled me, putting to rest all the other voices and the pain they brought.

Not true…
   lies…
   it was not real.
Your voice has now joined the others. You have become part of the voices of the past. You are one with them now.

Foolish, silly woman…
   he doesn't care…
   he didn't mean what he said…
   he played with you.
They scream louder, louder, louder.

Michele Spaccarotella

Make them stop…
  they laugh…
  they mock.
It wasn't true. No one will care again.

Hide me from these voices. Hide me from the pain
they inflict.
Shut down…
  that's the only way…
Lock away the heart.
Let no one see it ever again.

Maybe then the voices will stop, will cease to exist.
Maybe then you will too.

TRUSTING

I stopped trusting long ago.
I wouldn't let my heart believe.
Believing costs too much...
   the pain too great...
   the heart not able to endure the breaking.

So I wouldn't let it trust anymore.
It's easier that way.

And then I met you.
I resisted, you know...
   terrified my heart would feel those pains again;
   fearful those pieces, those fragile pieces,
      would shatter and break even more.

I don't know what it was...
   if it was the gentleness of your touch;
   or maybe it was the way your eyes looked at me
      and spoke unspoken words;
   or maybe it was the way your hand held mine in
      yours.

Whatever it was, I opened to you,
   and I let myself feel once more.
So many stirrings came to life,
   and with them, the trust I wouldn't let myself feel,
      returned.

Michele Spaccarotella

I trusted you…
  I believed you…
    and I felt you close to me.

My soul took on wings;
  soaring high and free.
My heart, fragile as it was, joined in.
High above the clouds, soaring heavenward;
  gliding gracefully on the promise of your words,
  I came alive.

You lied.

And like the bird with shattered wing,
  I plummeted;
    crashing to the earth below.
Broken, helpless and dying.

What could have possibly possessed me to ever imagine an interest from you?
What would make me think that two worlds, two very different worlds could merge?

What could I possibly give to you, as simple as I am?
What could a man of your distinction ever want from a woman like me?
What could I have been thinking to ever imagine anything like this?

Maybe it was the way your face lit up at seeing me, the way your mouth formed a smile, just for me.
Perhaps it was the happiness in your voice when you realized it was me on the phone.

It could have been the way your hand searched out and always found mine, how you held it so gently, so confidently, almost knowing I wouldn't pull away.

And then, it may have been your eyes, how they looked at me, how they held me and touched that place deep within, untouched for so very long, and how, with your eyes, you kissed me. Did you feel it?

There were the times you came close, so close that I could feel the rhythm of your breathing. I could feel your body touching mine.

Yes, it could have been that. It could have been any one of these. It was, perhaps all of these. But it was even more than this.

It was the music that my heart heard. It was the song sung sweetly by your words, that sang tenderly, promisingly to my fearful heart. Did you hear the music too?
Did your fingertips that softly touched my skin feel the trembling beneath them? Your smile said you did.

As I sit here now, tears falling like gentle drops of rain, a heart torn apart, I ask...
How could I ever have thought you cared for me, for you walked away, saying it wasn't true, leaving me standing here alone and confused.

For those things are things of fairy tales and make believe and movies, not real life.
Hearts cannot hear music, nor can eyes kiss another.
Fingertips touching cannot caress a heart hidden deep within.

In real life these things don't happen.

What could I have possibly been thinking?

ANOTHER LIFE

I lived another life so very long ago, a life so different,
a life so difficult to even remember.

The pages of memory so dusty, thick cobwebs
covering what once was.
Scenes filter through my mind like old photographs,
faded with time…
a smiling woman holding a baby in her arms…
a pretty little girl, delicate fingers wrapped
tightly in the hand of the woman…
a blonde headed boy, impish smile on his face…
children playing in the yard…
swings and sandboxes and tricycles…
birthday parties and presents at Christmas.

I turn more pages;
a home filled with the aroma of fresh baked
cookies…
children rushing in to grab them right from the
oven…
flowers growing in the yard, all colors of the
rainbow,
grown with love and patience…
smiles, hugs, laughter and love.

Michele Spaccarotella

I see this woman again;
   she is crying.
Sadness fill her eyes, her face and I know her heart
   is filled with much heartache.
There is something wrong.

There is a man here too.
He cannot see the heart of the woman;
   or maybe he chooses not to,
   for to see it means he would have to do something;
   something he perhaps wishes not to do.
So the woman cries alone.
And she keeps the aromas of a home;
   and she grows the flowers with love and patience;
   and she holds close the pretty little girl and
   the blonde headed boy.

The pages of memory are mostly torn and tattered
   now.
There is hurt and there is pain.
The love is gone,
   replaced with violence and anger.
The heart of love and patience has been ripped apart
   and trampled.
There are broken hearts, broken vows, broken bones
   and broken lives.
There is now a broken home.

The man screams angry insults;
   he laughs, he mocks.
The pretty little girl and the blonde headed boy

are grown;
they join in;
insult upon insult;
wound upon open wound;
piercing the heart,
  the heart of love and patience until…
Until there is no more.
And they wish she would leave.

No more home…
  no more life…
  no more heart…and no more love.
All that's left are broken pieces;
  pieces of what once was…
Too broken to be put together again.
Too shattered to be recognizable.
Too painful to go on.

So the woman walked away.
She took her tired and battered body,
  and she took her bruised and bleeding heart,
  and the pieces of herself that she could salvage.
She took the memory of the aroma of the cookies
  baking;
  and the flowers grown with love and patience.
She took the memory of the pretty little girl and
  the blonde headed boy,
  and she left behind what they had become.
She picked up these pieces as best as she could;
  and packed them away with the pieces that once
  were a heart…
And she left.

Michele Spaccarotella

She left it all behind;
   and entered a world she didn't know;
   and wondered if she wanted to be a part of.
She entered a life so foreign, so empty, so lonely;
   and she cried herself to sleep at night remembering…
   remembering the home, the aromas, the love and
      patience;
   and the pretty little girl and the blonde headed boy.

The woman has no home now;
   and sometimes the memory of one eludes her.
But she has in those pieces of her wounded heart the
   memory of all that was…
   and of the pretty little girl and the blonde headed
   boy.

And she struggles to go on;
   to put back together her life,
   a life she knows nothing of…
   a heart so damaged it seems beyond repair.
So she keeps it hidden,
   locked away…safe.

Time passes and some things begin to heal;
   and some things become a little easier.
I turn another page now
   and I see that the woman is smiling again.
Her broken bones have healed…
   but her eyes are sad still.
And her bruised and battered heart is nowhere to be
   seen, kept hidden…
Somewhere.

Out of nowhere comes the cancer.
With it comes the fear.
The disease overwhelms and terrifies her;
   the aloneness is enhanced.
And the old memories, the old hurts become real again.

The heart, that heart of love and patience from its
   hiding place somewhere deep within screams…
   screams out in agony…
   screams out in fear and anger;
   and tears, like giant raindrops flood the eyes
    of the woman until…

She meets the man.
The man who reaches out to her;
   who looks at her through eyes of compassion;
   who dares to boldly touch her and then reaches
    deep inside to find that hidden piece…
   the piece no one has touched;
   the piece no one has seen.
He has found.

He persists;
   and he pursues.
He feels so good;
   he feels so right.
And the woman
   who has so much pain;
   who is so fearful of even more…
Opens…slowly, delicately;
   one petal at a time

until she is in full bloom;
like the flowers in her garden
  grown with love and patience.

She has opened herself to this man.
As she fights this cancer
  she is ready to give her heart another chance,
  for he has given her that hope.
But the memories, those old photographs
  flood her once again.
Her heart, with the sweet fragrance of new life
  is ready…
  ready for a new chance with this new man.
But she doesn't forget the aroma of the cookies;
  or the flowers grown with love and patience;
  or the pretty little girl or the blonde headed boy.

She dances with this new man.
He will walk with her on this difficult journey.
He will hold her hand
  and be by her side.
The cancer has lost its power over her
  for her hand and her heart are safely held.

I see the woman weeping once more.
It has happened again.
The man has lied…
  and she cries.
Her heart is ripped apart,
  more violently than ever before.

She fights the cancer
  and she fights to survive.
She struggles to go on;
  and the woman holds tight to all she has left…
  the aroma of the cookies;
  the flowers grown with love and patience;
  the pretty little girl and the blonde headed boy.
And the man…
  who held her hand;
  who held her heart and
   touched her deep within.

Michele Spaccarotella

I'LL CALL

Like a schoolgirl when that special boy
   takes an interest in her
   I waited with giddy excitement
   for the phone to ring.

I thought I had heard wrong
   but you took out paper
   asking for my number
   saying you would call.

I waited,
   and every time the phone rang
   my heart fluttered.
You must be busy, I thought
   as the anticipation slowly
   turned to disappointment.

But then there you were
   making it all better
   saying we would talk
   and the excitement welled up again.

And oh, the things you said
   and oh, the way you looked
   and then you held me near.
So much better than a phone call,
   so well worth the wait.

I could see you now
    and hear what your face and your body spoke.
I could feel you
    and when you brought me back
    a second and third time,
    I could feel you surge through me.

But that schoolgirl innocence
    was played with
    for you didn't mean it.
You said it was a lie
    and I believed it all.

I'm not good enough
    you told me
I don't deserve respect
    and in your pompous arrogance
    no explanations are necessary
    for your agenda is more important
    than my pain.

But, you may protest
    these things you never said.
Ah, but yes you did.
You said all this and more.
Your silence spoke volumes.
Your silence broke my heart.

Michele Spaccarotella

YOU HAVE CANCER

In an instant, with just one word, your life comes to a
    halt, never to be the same again.
One word does this…cancer.
A word no one wants to hear.

You hear it, you hear nothing else.
And then you cry.
You cry at the unknown;
    you cry at the pain;
    you cry at what once was because nothing will ever be
       the same again.

Then you start your walk into the darkness, through the
    dark valley, or maybe it's a tunnel.
Either way, it's dark and you are terrified.
I've walked through this darkness called cancer and I
    have emerged on the other side…victorious.
I have come through, but not without scars, not without
    the wounds only cancer can bring.

I'm not the same person I was so very long ago.
In some ways I've become a new creation…the
    caterpillar that emerges from its cocoon, a gossamer
    winged butterfly…
    colorful, radiant, delicate, alive.
I am that butterfly.
I have been given new life.

But this new life did not come without a price…
   for everything we are given, something is taken in
   in return;
   for joy to be, there must be sorrow and pain;
   for the rainbow to come, there must be storm clouds.

The wounds of cancer run deep.
And in the darkness of this valley…
   in the midst of this storm…
   a ray of light, of hope, a hand;
   the rainbow…you.
Your hand reached out and lifted me up.

Did the cancer also make you run?

AWAKENED

My heart has been awakened, awakened from a very deep sleep. The pain that was kept far away by this sleep has now returned. Like the fairy tale beauty who was awakened by a kiss, my heart has been awakened by a touch. But unlike the fairy tale, there seems to be no happy ending. For the heart that slept to escape the pain has now been awakened to experience more.

There are moments of tenderness when eyes meet, when hands reach out and fingers touch, when hearts seem to speak without words. And yet they are only moments, so fleeting, so far between. In these moments a gentleness surrounds me, a gentleness like no other. And then it is gone and the pain returns to fill the emptiness.

Your words cut like a knife, stabbing pains in the heart. My heart screams out, "why, why did you do this? Why did you awaken me from my sleep? Why did you so gently touch me?"

I wonder why I let you awaken me. Should I let my heart stay or should I let it sleep once more, for it is in sleep that your words have no effect on it. It is in sleep that the pain loses its icy grip. But in my heart now you will always remain, even should it sleep again.

SOMETIMES

Sometimes in life we become lucky and we meet someone who touches us, someone who awakens that which has been asleep for so very long.

Sometimes…but not always.

Sometimes in life two people going in different directions on very different paths find these paths crossing, and they meet, but they don't know why.

Sometimes…but not always.

Sometimes these two paths can become one, when souls are touched and words can be believed and promises are true.   Then hopes are raised and possibilities begin to emerge.

Sometimes…but not always.

Sometimes the hurt comes and compassion vanishes. Attempts to right the wrongs fall on deaf ears and hard hearts. Then one cries and one walks away.

And sometimes…becomes most times.

Why did you enter the chamber
   where the wounded heart sleeps…

Why did you gently awaken it
   with your touch…

Why did you hold it in your hands
   caressing it softly with your words…

Why did you enter the chamber
   if you did not intend to stay?

HIDDEN SANCTUARY

Can you tell me where broken hearts go? Can you tell me where they run and hide, where they can escape the memories that they hold so dear, those memories that cause so much pain?

Is there such a place, for if there is, my heart surely needs to find it.

A safe place, a place of comfort, where the heart can rest, where it knows that no one can hurt it again.
A place where, for awhile at least, it can stop, it need not be strong, and it can allow the tears to fall unhindered, unafraid of what others may think.

Is there such a place, for my heart needs to be there?

A place where pain doesn't exist, where the sting of false hopes and illusions have lost their power.
A place where hearts and heart pieces can be mended, if that is at all possible.
A place to rest and to feel no more.

Is there such a place? I think not.

I fear that perhaps this heart, this broken and bleeding heart must find its own hidden sanctuary, its own cave, its own tomb and bury itself within the cold, dark dampness.

Michele Spaccarotella

It is in this cave, the cave of the heart, where hopefully your memory will not find it, where your touch will not still be felt after all this time, where your eyes will not penetrate to its very depth, its very being. It is this cave which will entomb my heart and protect it.

Is this possible? I fear not.

I feel your touch
  like silk gliding over bare skin.
And I wonder how it could move me so.

Your presence,
  how could it excite me as it has.
You, who I hardly know,
  you have penetrated the walls around my heart.
You have torn down my fortress,
  conquered my refuge, my hiding place.

How?
How could you have done this?

Your words,
  flowing easily over lips smiling for me.
Words...words that encouraged me to trust;
  to continue to tear down what remained of that wall.
It all came so easy for you,
  and I found how easy it became to trust you.

How?
How could you have done this?

And now the walls are down...
  destroyed.
You have left me open;
  vulnerable, defenseless.
I try to cover myself from your words that hurt,
  piercing my heart.
But the walls are gone
  and cannot hide my woundedness.

I thought you were different.
I thought I could trust you.
I thought you wouldn't hurt me
   because your touch was so gentle;
   your words seemed so sincere;
   nothing to make me think otherwise.

How?
How could you have done this?

I thought you were different.
But as I stand here,
   trying to hide from the harshness,
   the cruelty of your words,
I realize that in the end
   your touch…unreal;
   your words…empty;
   your talk…cheap;
           and
   my heart…destroyed.

The truth only sets us free if we willing embrace it.
If we shut the door, we lock ourselves in the prison
called denial.

Some of the greatest blessings, the greatest gifts come
in the ordinary and quiet times of our lives, when we
reach out to touch another person, when we open our
hearts to the love that can be shared.

Love often escapes us.
It comes quietly, dressed in poverty,
   clothed in humility,
   wrapped in simplicity.
Then we run and hide our heart from what we
   desire most, for fear.
And after it's gone,
   the heart softly weeps.

DARK ROADS AND STRANGERS

I met a man once on a very dark and frightening road. It was a road I had never traveled and one I didn't want to be on. I had no choice, for the road was chosen for me. The road was called cancer, and I was traveling it alone.

Dark roads can be dangerous and one must be wary of strangers, and even though there was something about him, something different, comforting, and he seemed so kind, so caring, so sensitive, this man I met was still a stranger.

So I was cautious. I had to be, traveling alone like I was. I needed to protect myself and I needed to keep my eyes on the road ahead because dark roads can be very dangerous, and strangers can be too.

As I traveled along, I began to notice it wasn't quite as dark as it had been. In that new light I came to see that I wasn't alone and that my hand was being held along the way. That man, that stranger was there with me and as we traveled in the darkness that wasn't quite as dark as it had been, he spoke.

He spoke words so sweet and he spoke directly to my heart. And he never let go of my hand. But I was still cautious, nonetheless, for strangers along dark roads can be very dangerous.

Days went by and still he traveled by my side and spoke those same sweet words and he always found my hand to hold snugly in his. And the darkness continued to get lighter and lighter, until one day I saw it wasn't dark anymore.

It was gloriously bright, brilliant, shining and that man, that stranger, was somehow more familiar. I was comfortable with him, safe with him. He smiled and spoke of more to come, yes, he promised of more to come. And even though I still did not know where the road was going, it wasn't that bad because of him and the light that he brought.

He walked close to me and at times I could feel his embrace. The winding curves of the road called cancer and the steep hills and bumps did not frighten as before, as long as he was there.

Then one day a dark cloud hung overhead and the wind blew fiercely and the road was difficult to see. The rain beat down in torrents and blinded me, blinded me so, that I didn't realize it wasn't rain, but giant teardrops and the thunder I thought I heard wasn't thunder, but the harshness of his words. And that wind, no, it wasn't wind, it was him rushing past me, leaving me alone again.

In time the rain became a little gentler and the wind less strong but the dark cloud continued to obscure and the road was once again dark and frightening. And the man, who once was a stranger, became a stranger once more and was nowhere to be found.

One must be careful of dark roads and strangers. They both can be very dangerous.

Flowers are dying.
colorful petals falling to the ground
like silently shed tears.

Around them, the great oak
standing majestically,
drops its leaves one by one
slowly falling until, naked it stands.

Warm breezes suddenly turn cool
chilling winds rustle
the crisp, dry leaves as they fall.

The sun sinks in the west
down…down it goes
crimson shades reflected in its journey
then…darkness.

Winter will soon be here,
its cold, icy chill
ravaging the nakedness all around.

I stand now like that oak
naked and exposed to the coldness,
stripped bare by your words.

Michele Spaccarotella

I have shed my petals like the flowers
and my sun has reached its destination.
It has journeyed down,
for you have taken it away.

I stand in sorrow
as the wind buffets me.

FOOLISH

Oh, how foolish you must think me to be,
  how naïve to the ways of the world.
Perhaps we play by different rules.

Was that all it was,
  a game you played with me?
Were you just passing the time?

But you see
  I wasn't playing.
For me, it wasn't a game;
  it was real.

And while you played
  I slowly gave to you my heart;
  opening to your touch, your smile, your gaze.

Oh, how foolish you must think me to be.
For all the while you were playing
  I was slowly, slowly falling,
  falling to a place where broken hearts
    and broken lives dwell.

Oh, how foolish you must think me to be,
  trusting, believing, stepping out in hope,
    hoping beyond hope;
    trusting beyond trust.

Michele Spaccarotella

Taking a chance, finding no reason not to.
Fearing...
   yet somehow feeling safety surround me.
Falling...
   slowly falling...
     into that pit where broken hearts and
     broken lives dwell.

Oh, how foolish you must think me to be.

When the storm of cancer surrounded me, the raging wind of anger, the crashing waves of depression, your hand came through and found mine.

The wind that raged became a gentle breeze that caressed, the waves that crashed, threatening to drown became as soft kisses upon the sand.

You calmed the waters and made my heart tranquil. I was not afraid of the dark for the dark had become light in the grasp of your hand holding mine. And sunshine and warmth filled my heart to overflowing and radiated outward.

Do you know what you held within
   your hands,
   a heart, a life
   so fragile, so afraid.
You held that, did you know?

You held within those gentle hands
   a part of me no one has touched,
   for you see I never wanted
   to give that away
   to anyone…ever again.
I hid it, not very well, I guess.
I would let no man see that place
Until you.

I don't know how.
I don't know why,
   but you found it.
And I didn't know you,
   yet I felt that I did.
And I wanted the chance
   to know even more,
   was promised that,
   when you found that part of me,
   with just a touch, with just a look
   it was yours and I knew
   those gentle hands would not harm.

So to you I gave that part of me
   I would never give away again.
Because I knew or thought I knew
   within your care
   it would be safe.

Oh, how deceived one can be,
   the games that can be played
   for that precious part of me you held
   meant nothing to you.
And when you were done playing
   you just tossed it aside.
But that was a life, a spirit
   that you let die.

I pick up this heart,
   this heart so bruised.
I try to comfort,
   but the hurt too raw.
I look once again for a hiding place,
   one much better than before.
And I make a vow
   this heart won't be found.
By tender hands,
   that touch and hold;
By eyes of passion,
   that search the depths.
By words of promise,
   that are sung so sweet.

Never again, I vow
   as I try to bury this heart so deep.

Love…the investment into eternity.
The only thing that lasts.
The only thing we leave behind and also take with us.

❦

Love may be closer to you than you imagine;
you just must be willing to take a step.

❦

Life devoid of love is no life at all.

You gave me hope...
    when you knew there was none.

You gave me a song...
    when there was no reason to sing.

You spoke words so sweet...
    when you knew that they were empty.

You took away the darkness...
    when you knew it would only return.

You took me by the hand...
    and you flew me to the heavens
    when you knew you wouldn't stay
    and I couldn't fly alone
    and by your leaving, death was imminent
    because the broken-winged bird cannot fly.

Michele Spaccarotella

HERO

I thought you were my hero.
I thought you came to save…
   to save me from the cancer;
   to save me from the emptiness;
   to save me from the pain.

You walked right in and took control.
You confused me at first.
But then I guess that's what heroes do…
   they forge ahead;
   they take control;
   they rescue those in distress.

You stirred something inside me.
And my fears were strong;
   but your tenderness was stronger.

You were awakening feelings I didn't
   want to feel again;
   the pain of losing them is much too great.
So I resisted.
Did you know that?

I kept my broken heart hidden;
   yet it was found.
Heroes do that too, I guess.
You persisted…
   and you won.
You marched right in;
   and you found that secret place.

And when I stopped my fighting
  and I let you win my heart.
When I took down the walls
  or maybe it was you who conquered them.
When my heart lay open and exposed
  when my heart lay trustingly in your hands;
You, my hero...
  squeezed the life out of it...
  left it bleeding and dying...
  writhing in the pain of your words.

I thought you were my hero.
And heroes always win the heart.

The harshness of you words
leave me with the bitter taste of sour wine
so unlike the sweetness you once gave to me.

The vast blackness calls to me,
  beckons me to become one with it.
Chilling, empty, extending forever;
  no end to be seen.

It calls me, as if to come home.

What would my life be like
  if I had never met you,
  if our paths had never crossed?
Would I have been better off not meeting you at all?

My heart would say
  it never would have broken,
  and it never would have cried,
  and it wouldn't feel the pain that never goes away.

And all that's true
  if I never would have met you.

But then I would have missed your touch,
  as soft as a whisper.
And I would have missed
  the wings you gave my heart and
  the way it soared to the heavens when you were
    near.
I would have missed the twinkling stars and
  the dancing moonbeams.

My ears would not have heard
  the sweetness of your words,
  soft melodies like angel voices.
And I would have missed the dance,
  when we came together, face to face,
  an embrace, a gaze,
  a rhythm felt by both of us.

I would have missed all that,
  if I never would have met you.

So I tell my heart
  to stop its crying
  and to push the pain aside
  for it was blessed for a moment in knowing you
  and having those wings to fly
  and to feel your embrace as you danced with me.

And how I would have missed all that,
  if I never would have met you.

ANYWAY

I didn't want you close to me
   I was afraid, you know;
Afraid of what I would feel…
Afraid of what I would lose…
But you came close…anyway.

I didn't want you to touch me
   because I wanted it so much;
Or to find what I had hidden…
Or to open the door that would not shut again…
But you touched…anyway.

I didn't want to believe the words you spoke
   fearing they were empty;
That they would stir my heart…
That they would promise so much…
But I believed you…anyway.

I didn't want to dance with you
   to have your eyes look so deeply into mine;
   to look and speak to my soul…
To hold your hand and let you lead me…
I feared so much because
   I wanted more.
But you danced with me…anyway.

I accepted all you gave to me
  because I wanted to.
Hesitant, fearful,
  yet I accepted.
And when I passed that point of no return,
  when my fears were gone…
  when I returned your gaze…
  when I thought I could believe your words…
That's when it came;
  the thing I feared most…
  the betrayal of my heart
  and the pain I was so afraid of
  was now a part of me.
Because I let you in…anyway.

I tried to reach you one more time
  to touch that heart turned hard;
  to spark the compassion that I know is there
  buried so deep within your heart.

My fears have become reality.
I received no response.
I guess if you ignore it enough
  it never really exists
  and maybe it will go away.

But you see, I do exist
  or did you forget that fact?
I'm a person, and I hurt and I bleed…
  and I break.

I know that you heard what I had to say.
It was written all over your face.
And your refusal to deal with it suggests
  perhaps the truth is hard to hear.

I did not mean to hurt you.
God knows I told you so.
I tried so many times
  and I gave my apologies
  and accepted responsibility.

I just wanted to be acknowledged
  to be treated with respect,
  for to be ignored is worse;
  for to be ignored says that I don't exist

and I never was
and we both know
that isn't true.

For there was something.
I'm certain of that.
But it made you run
and become afraid to speak
and hide within yourself.

So in the wake of your destruction
my heart continues to bleed
for all that was,
and never was;
for all that was said,
and never said;
for all that could be,
and now is lost.

And I try to stop the bleeding
and I try to ease the pain.
I close my eyes
and I see your face once again.
And I feel you close beside me.
a hand holding mine so tight.
I see your eyes look into mine,
and I feel this death one more time.

Yes, I tried to reach you one more time.
to touch that heart turned hard.
But you turned against me
and broke what was left of a heart.

Your touch…like the early morning dew
　that softly kisses the rose;
　the breeze that tickles the leaves,
　setting them aflutter.

I heard you with the ears of my heart.
Love teaches us this.

In the quiet, in the stillness the heart speaks.
Do we dare to listen?

Michele Spaccarotella

How so like a man, you chose to end
That which you yourself had started
Few words, no reasons
Short and to the point
No chance for me to speak
You were in charge
Less likely that way for me
To make a scene, I guess
But you should know me better than that.

How so like a man
To knowingly touch the heart of a woman
Knowing her circumstances
And yet moving beyond
Purposely touching and awakening.

And then with masculine cunning
The way you chose to end it
To walk away
Aware that my heart was broken and crying
But caring not
For the game that was played was over.

How so like a man
To protect yourself at a woman's expense
Turning your back
Turning your eyes
Refusing to see now
My heart that cries.

God! What an ending!
So like a man
To care only of himself
And leave the wounded behind.

ALONE

Alone in my room at night, behind the safety of closed doors and pulled shades, I gaze at myself and wonder what it is about me that made you hurt me so.
I stand before the mirror and wonder if perhaps you found the ugliness and damage from cancer, repulsive. Maybe because of this, you see me as less of a woman.

And then I cry.

I wonder, too, if you think that I am not good enough for you, my mind not as brilliant, my education so much less, my conversation, dull. Maybe you think our worlds are so very far apart and many things separate them, the quietness and simplicity of mine, the busyness and prestige of yours. Could they ever merge?

And then I cry.

My mind comes alive then with thoughts of all that passed. I remember when I felt your arms around me, the comfort and warmth of your embrace. I remember the way you tilted your head, ever so slightly, to accept the kiss I tenderly placed upon your cheek. I see the times you couldn't contain the happiness that shown in your face when you saw me, or the joy I heard in your voice.

And then I become confused at the ease with which you did all this, and then said it wasn't true. And I wonder what it was I did or what it is I am that made you hurt me so.

And then I cry.

As the tears continue to flow and the hurt continues to hurt, I find no answers have come, no solace from the pain. I do not believe that you meant to hurt me, for if you did, that would make you a cruel and evil man, and I know that you are not. Yet by doing what you have done, that is how you are acting and it is so very opposite that which I first saw in you.
And I wonder what it was I did or what it is I am that made you hurt me so.

And then I cry.

Something happened, of that much I'm sure, to make you turn like you did. The tenderness and compassion seem so very far away, almost surreal. Yet I know they happened. The joy, the happiness, the warmth are gone, replaced with a cold, stony heart.
I gaze at myself once more and I wonder what it was I did or what it is I am that made you hurt me so.

And then I cry.

Michele Spaccarotella

A WOMAN KNOWS

A woman knows when a man is interested in her,
  when he seeks something more.
She can see it in his eyes…
  the way they look at her…
  the way they reach to the depths of her soul
    and touch that special place…
  the way they hold her eyes.
It is almost as if he were caressing her, kissing her.
And if the woman is interested in return,
  she lifts the veil that hides and leaves herself
    exposed and vulnerable…
    open to the man.
A woman knows this.

She knows also by the way he comes close to her…
  the way he crosses over those boundaries we all have,
    those limits we need and set for ourselves.
Yet he crosses over them even before he's invited.
He steps over these boldly and so…
A woman knows this.

A woman knows by the way he touches her,
  in ways that become familiar over time
    and yet no time has passed, for this is all so new.
But still he touches…
  and he does this with an ease, in a manner so
    comfortable, almost knowing she will welcome him.
A woman knows this.

A woman knows by his words
  and by the tone of his voice.
Her ears hear these words meant just for her…
  they come without hesitation,
  they come spontaneously
   and the excitement in his voice gives himself away.
His words entice her…
  they promise of more to come…
  and they encourage her to trust him.
And because they come so easily,
  she knows they must come from his heart.
A woman knows this.

She can tell when he holds her hand
  and feels hers within his.
It feels as if they fit together,
  like a hand in a glove…
  one covering the other…
  snug, but not tight…
  becoming one.
And she feels more.
She feels something surge through her,
  through these hands holding…
  feels a force that goes straight to her heart.
She wonders if he feels the same
  and knows he does without having to ask.
A woman knows this.

And when all of this comes together…
  the way his eyes hold at the same time
   his hand holds…
  the way he dares to come close and smiling,
   he touches her tenderly, suggestively, she knows.

She knows without a doubt.
And her body trembles…
And her body aches…
And her heart reaches out to his,
 to become one;
 to touch his soul;
 and fly to the heavens.
A woman knows this.

So if she knows all this.
If her heart and her soul
 spoke to his heart and soul;
If she knew…
 and he knew.
Why, pray tell, why did he run?
Why did he leave?
And why doesn't she know why?
Did he become scared?
Did hearts speak words
 they were not prepared to hear?

And the woman who knew
 realizes she doesn't know a thing.
And she weeps.

You took liberties that weren't
  yours to take;
You crossed the line that separated us.
You decided to do this, not I;
  and because of your power,
  you did as you pleased.

But I welcomed you
  because of a thing called trust.
And because of the cancer
  I believed it was sincere,
  for who could deceive
  with something like this.

But it wasn't;
  it was your power over mine
  to do as you pleased.
A power to take advantage
  of a heart and a trust…
  of a spirit and a life,
  with no regard for the outcome or
  the hurt that you would leave behind.

You did as you pleased.
You said what you wanted.
And when you were done
  you walked away
  and you didn't look back.
No need to explain
  for the one who has the power
  is the one who makes the rules
  and the other must play by them.

So you came close to me
   and you suggested more.
And encouraged me to believe you
   and all the while it was only a game.
And when you were done,
   you claimed the victory
   and walked away for
   the game was over.

And I, the loser, lost more
   than the game.
For you broke a trust;
   you broke a spirit;
   you broke a heart.

I saw you today
   and my heart skipped a beat;
   and my body trembled;
   and I wondered if you noticed.

You let me pass by,
   the perfect gentleman that you are.
I tried to catch your gaze,
   but you averted your eyes from me.

Did you hear the sadness in my voice
   when I politely thanked you?
Did you see the tears in my eyes
   as I passed by?

I wanted you to stop me
   to say something…anything,
   to make me feel worthwhile.
Yet instead, I was made to feel
   as if I were invisible.

I wanted to come to you
   and ask you why.
But you know how frightened I am of you
   and I didn't want to make a scene.
I didn't know how you would act.

Michele Spaccarotella

I wanted to touch your hand,
   the hand that used to hold mine
   and tell you how good it felt.
But I was afraid you would pull away.
You don't want to be near me.

I wondered if your eyes
   followed as I passed by.
I hoped they did.
And I wanted to turn, just to see
   but fear of being disappointed prevented me,
   so I continued and cried silently on the inside
   for a missed opportunity.

I save the real tears
   for the night, when sleep doesn't come
   and the pillow is damp,
   I remember once again.

And I wish you would have stopped me.
And I wish I would have touched you.
And that our eyes would have met
   and maybe you would have spoken.

I saw you today
   and my heart skipped a beat.

THE MEETING

The woman met the man when she was in a very dark place.
She was alone and this place frightened her.
She didn't want to be here, but she had no choice.

She had no reason to believe the man, yet she had every reason to.
When one is in a dark place such as this it is difficult to believe another would deceive.
But she was still reluctant to trust, she had had so much hurt already and she was so terrified of more.

Yet the man seemed so kind, so caring, how could she not trust.
He was so gentle with her as he stepped in to help light the way and to help take away her pain.

She thought he could be a hero…her hero.
She could see how this could be so and she heard the words he spoke about wanting to be there.
Yes, he was a hero.
He would take away her pain.
And she wondered if he was the one she had been waiting for.

So she dared to take a chance.
And she let herself feel and she let herself begin to trust because he was too good to hurt her.
She let him see that place she kept hidden from others.

And she let him take her to a place she never thought she would see.

The woman let herself dream again and she wanted to be near the man, just wanting to be close to him.
She wanted him to hold her and she wanted him to kiss away her pain.

The man made her smile again.
He brought joy and laughter and he gave her hope.
The man said he wanted to share more with her and when he said this, he brought so much sunshine into that dark place.

Oh, the joy the woman felt.
She came alive and he gave her reason to celebrate.
The woman tried to imagine what all this would be like, but she couldn't because it was more than she could ever hope for.
The dark place was now brilliant.

But one day, the woman saw that darkness again and she began to worry.
The man was there and he was in the darkness and that's what frightened her even more, for he was never dark, he was always light.

The man spoke to the woman and as he did, like a fast approaching storm, the darkness soon covered her as well.
She found herself in that dark place once again.

His words weren't kind.
They cut and they pierced her heart and her soul and she felt the life he had given her slowly being drained out of her.

The man would speak no more.
He turned and he walked away and she was cast by the wayside.
Her hero, the one who would save her from the pain now brought her more pain.

The woman tried to find the man, but she couldn't.
She saw a man that looked like him but when she tried to speak to him, she realized it wasn't he.
This man was hard, cold, distant, so unlike that warm and gentle man she knew.

The woman continues to search for him, hoping one day she will find him again.
She still sees the man that looks like him and she wonders if he knows where her hero has gone.
But she is too afraid to speak to him.
She tried that once and he was not too kind to her for her to take that chance again.
He was cruel to her and her made her cry.

The woman wonders if the man knows that she waits for him, hoping he will return.
She waits on the path they both walked once, hand in hand, until he got off.

Michele Spaccarotella

The woman waits for the man who brought her sunshine and laughter, who let her dream again, and who took away her pain.

She doesn't think she will find him, but she waits still because...
She misses him.

In the darkness of the cancer a light shone.
It came unexpectedly,
  it came suddenly.
You brought the sunshine into this darkness of
  death, into the stench.

Like the bird with song to sing,
  and wings to fly,
  I flew heavenward,
  carefree...
My heart sang and my wings took flight.

Oh, what life you brought to me.

The things I've heard said about you
  must be true.
And yet I never saw them before.
Because the man I met was a different man,
  different from the one I see before me now.

He was warm and caring,
  not cold and hard.
He was sensitive and kind,
  not harsh and indifferent.
He was someone I trusted,
  not someone I was afraid of.
And he treated me with dignity and respect,
  not as if I were invisible.

Because the man I met
  was not the same man I see before me now.
And I wonder where he went,
  and why he ran away.
And what it was that made him change.
Because the man I met I cared for and
  thought he cared for me.

Then I wonder how a person can inflict
   so much pain on another,
   or how responsibility can be denied,
   pretending like nothing happened.
And how they can crush the spirit
   and break a heart
   and never look back.

Yes, the man I met was a different man
   than the man I see before me now.

YOUR WORLD

You go about your life
  in your world,
  so far removed from mine.

So removed from the words you spoke
  and the hand you held;
  from the promises you made
  and the heart you broke.

And you go about your life
  because these don't concern you.
You changed your mind
  and you walked away.

No reasons are needed
  because your world is different.
And your power is mightier,
  and you can do as you please
  to gentle souls and trusting hearts.
Because their world is different from yours.

So you play your games.
  and you win a heart.
  and when you're done
  you show no concern
  for the damage you've caused.

You don't look back
  or show any care
  for the broken heart,
  or the shattered trust,
  or the tears that are falling.

For your world is different
  from the world that I'm in,
  and broken hearts
  and broken lives
  don't matter much to you.

Michele Spaccarotella

I was good enough to touch
   to be sought out time and again;
To hold a hand;
To hold a look with eyes so deep.
And then was sent away.

But now it's as if I don't exist
   as if I never was.
Not a word to help ease this pain.
For I'm gone now…
   just not good enough anymore.

Do you ever wish you could start anew
    and leave the past behind;
    with someone you could get to know,
    someone who would take the time?

Where you wouldn't have to worry
    if the words you heard were true
    and the deeds that were done would not bring fear
    that it all might hurt you.

Where honesty and truthfulness
    were something to hold high
    and hearts would never fear
    that they would break and cry.

I thought that when I met you
    these things I saw in you;
    that you would not mislead me
    and that your words were true.

Oh, how wrong I guess I was
    how silly and naïve;
    your words were false, your deeds were too
    and I was so deceived.

Michele Spaccarotella

MIDDLE OF THE NIGHT

In the middle of the night
   when sleep doesn't come
   I cry out in anguish and pain.
I walk the memories of my mind
   and it is your memory that haunts me.

"Leave me be," I cry.
"Why do you haunt me still?"
"Why won't you let me heal this brokenness?"
"Leave my heart."
But you don't listen;
   you don't leave.
You stay.

And then the heart remembers…
   the smiles
   the embraces
   the joy and laughter you brought to me.

In the middle of the night
   when sleep doesn't come
   I feel your hand in mine.
   "Go away," I plead.
   "Let me be."
But you linger, you tease and
   and you won't let me forget.
"But you don't want me, it was all a game."

I try to understand why you did this to me,
   why you said what wasn't true.
And how you could turn your back on me
   knowing the pain that would follow.

In the middle of the night
   when sleep doesn't come...
I cry.

Michele Spaccarotella

Why didn't you just keep your distance?
Why did you have to come so close?
Why did you let your words
  be heard by the ears of my heart?
Why did you let your eyes look
  through the windows to my soul?

Why didn't you just keep your distance,
  for you knew what was at stake,
  a heart, a soul, a life,
  that could so easily break?
Why did you have to come so close,
  then run away like you did?

If you knew you wouldn't stay,
  if you knew you shouldn't touch,
  why then, why didn't you just keep your distance
  from this heart that learned to trust?

And if you knew these things
  and knew this heart believed;
  why then did you give it
  the wings to set it free?
If you knew you wouldn't stay;
  if you knew that you deceived.

But since you did come close and touch
  and didn't stay away;
  could you not have at least found
  someway to say.

That you didn't mean to hurt,
 you didn't mean to lie;
 that you should have kept your distance;
 you should not have come so close.

Could you not have shown compassion,
 given me some respect?
For you came across that distance
 and you opened the door so wide.
You left my heart so exposed
 with nowhere to hide.

Could you not at least show courage
 to right the wrong you did?
When you robbed me of my dignity
 and shattered a heart that started to live.
Because you didn't keep your distance.
Because you came close and touched.

We didn't have much time together,
   nor did we speak of many things.
But I felt your arms around me,
   and the comfort a hand can bring.

But the things we shared said so much,
   that I didn't have to be afraid.
Then I found that you were gone,
   oh, how I wish you had stayed.

What was it that made you run,
   that made you lie and deceive,
That made you say the things you did,
   that made my heart believe?

No, we didn't have much time together,
   that much I know is true.
My only hope is that you know,
   how much I cared and now miss you.

FIRST SIGHT

I never believed in love at first sight;
I still don't know if I do.
But something happened to me
   the day that I met you.

Something so different, so out of place;
I wondered if you felt it too.
And then I saw that look on your face
   and that is when I knew.

Something had passed between us;
   maybe when you held my hand,
   or maybe when you caught my eye.
And as time went on, it would intensify.

I thought I had been given a new chance;
To live, to love, to sing and dance,
   with someone special, with someone who
   would be there with me, to see me through.

But then you changed, you grew cold
   and I wondered what I had done.
What did I say, what did I do
   to make you want to run?

You didn't give me answers,
   you wouldn't tell my heart;
What it was that made you leave,
   that made you want to part.

Michele Spaccarotella

Did you fear what was at stake
 or were you in too deep?
So you chose to leave, to walk away,
 to make my heart break and weep.

But something passed between us;
 that much I know is true.
Something so different, so out of place
 the day that I met you.

So should you ever change your mind
 and want to start anew,
I shouldn't be too hard to find,
I'm in that place, where I first met you.

Heaven sent you to me
a warm embrace to walk by my side;
and like the whisper of angel's wings
your touch left me feeling
safe and cared for.

Your words, sweet melodies, played the strings of
my heart and in time,
my heart sang sweetly the new song you had given me.

In the stillness, in the quiet,
the voice of the heart speaks.
It speaks with a whisper,
with a touch,
with a glance.
In the noise of the world
one cannot hear these words.
They can only be heard in the quiet.

Michele Spaccarotella

NO GOOD-BYE

We met at a place so difficult.
We met at a place so dark.
It was a journey I had to be on,
   one on which I didn't want to embark.

But I had to go forward, one step at a time,
   into the dark I feared.
You would be there, you told me so,
   standing close, so very near.

As time went on we traveled
   and you were by my side.
Your shoulder was there to lean on
   and that look was in your eyes.

And then one day it happened,
   from out of the blue it came.
Not a word was true, you told me.
I was shattered, it was only a game.

A game that you had played with me
   in this place so very dark.
Now I had to walk alone
   and my life was falling apart.

For you gave me false hopes and illusions.
You gave me reason to dream.
That when this walk was over,
 when this journey done;
 we would find ourselves on another,
 one that had just begun.

But it was all over, you told me;
 it was all just a lie.
And you turned to go and left me
 and you never said good-bye.

Michele Spaccarotella

REASONS

I guess you had your reasons
　of which I'll never know;
How a man with such compassion
　could hurt another so.

For you told me that you cared
　and you wanted to be there;
And when I turned to reach for you
　you had disappeared.

You said it wasn't true,
　that they were empty words;
But it wasn't just the words you spoke
　that my heart had heard.

It was the way you looked at me,
　the way your eyes held mine;
The way you touched and held my hand,
　the way they both entwined.

But then you left
　without much talk;
You wouldn't tell me why.
And all I can do is tell
　my hurting heart not to cry.

So I guess you had your reasons
　of which I'll never know;
Why you touched, why you looked
　and then you chose to go.

THE GIFT

I gave to you a gift one time
  a gift that I chose with care.
A gift from my heart, a gift to say
  I'm glad we met along the way.

But it seems that made you angry
  and you refused to even speak.
And you tried to give it back to me
  my gift you wouldn't keep.

So you cast aside that gift I gave
  and a part of me went too.
For I chose that gift from my heart
  a gift from me to you.

I have no idea what you did with it,
  that gift that I chose with care.
But I know that day you cast it aside,
  a part of me was shattered and died.

Because I gave that gift to you,
  a gift that I chose with care.
A gift from my heart, a gift to say,
  I'm glad we met along the way.

They say that time heals all wounds.
Of that I'm not so sure.

Perhaps they heal on the outside;
   perhaps they just become numb.
They never go away.

And the people that inflict these,
   what about them?
They stay with us
   embedded somewhere just beneath the surface.

And when least expected,
   when healing is thought to have occurred,
   they break through
   and they bleed into our lives once more.

If we could leave the past behind
   and start again today;
And if I heard you say the words
   that you would find a way.

To take away the sadness
   to dry the tears I shed;
To say you'd like to try that walk,
   not knowing what lies ahead.

Then I would open wide my arms
   and draw you close to me;
And dare to dream once again
   and let my heart fly free.

So if you ever think there could
   be even the slightest chance;
Come…just take my hand in yours
   and ask me once more to dance.

Alone at night, the pain consumes me,
   it brings me to my knees.
I scream out in anguish and
   I scream to the Heavens
   and I scream to the Creator of all.

"Why?"
"Why do you let these things happen?"

And then the pain washes over me and
   tears flood my eyes.
I am tossed about like angry waves crashing
   against the shore.
Over and over I'm hurled,
   beaten down,
   drowning in the hurt until
   I find myself safely brought to shore.

When there is no more to cry
   and the silence surrounds
   then and only then,
   is the answer to be heard.

"My child, I feel your pain as well
   and my heart breaks along with yours.
But whose heart is it that breaks the most,
   the one who receives the pain
   or the one by whose hand
   that pain has been inflicted?
My heart breaks along with that heart too.
For no one wins when matters of
   broken hearts are at stake."

I wasn't looking for you, you know,
I wasn't seeking to find you.
I was minding my own life
   and I thought you were minding yours.

Because I wasn't looking for you,
   you took me by surprise.
Maybe you even took yourself by surprise
   that happens too, you know.

Here, in the middle of our lives
   we found each other,
   both of us not prepared for what would happen.
But then who ever is
   when heart speaks to heart.

Like the fragrance after a sudden
   spring shower or;
   the sweet song sung by the lark or;
   the budded rose bursting forth with color;
I came alive.

I wasn't looking for you, you know,
   nor was I seeking to find you.
We met unexpectedly
   on a magical path;
   a path that led to…
Nowhere.

Michele Spaccarotella

TRUTH

When one has power
   they believe they can do what they want;
   they can say what they want;
   because power means that they can.

But I do not believe that is what power is.

I believe that truth is power,
   to live the truth;
   to speak the truth;
   to look another in the eye because
     one has nothing to hide.
That is power.
And when one can do that,
   one is powerful.

Because therein lies the truth
   and that truth is power.
One need nothing else but truth.

One is truly powerful when one holds truth.

JUST A LITTLE

You stood just a little too close…
You looked just a little too deep…
You touched just a little too much.

And it set my heart to thinking
    set me to wondering why.
Yet I didn't want to believe
    I was so afraid of the lie.

But I did.
Because…

You stood just a little too close…
You looked just a little too deep…
You touched just a little too much.

You set my heart on fire
    with the words you chose to say.
And then one day I found
    that you had gone away.

I tried to find you to ask you why
    to ask you to please explain.
But you wouldn't talk, you wouldn't look
    at this heart in so much pain.

I try to go on as best as I can
    with no reasons to be revealed.
And I wonder if this broken heart
    will ever be healed.

Then I cry.
Because…

You stood just a little too close…
You looked just a little too deep…
You touched just a little too much.

Be careful with words,
   they are very powerful.
They hold the power to give life
   and they hold the power to take life.

Words are life giving or life taking.
The choice lies within your heart.

Sometimes it is the things we do not say that
   wound another more than the things we do say.

The scars on the outside come nowhere near
   the scars on the inside.
The pain of the heart never goes away.
The anguish and the tears continue to come;
   weeping…always weeping.

Michele Spaccarotella

A CUP OF COFFEE

I invited you for a cup of coffee
"I'd like that," is what you said.
Little did I know that day that
   I was being misled.

A simple cup of coffee
   some talk, just you and me.
But I would soon come to know
   the words you spoke were empty.

You smiled when you said them
   and you looked me in the eyes.
Then you brought me close to you
   and I will always wonder why.

Why you would say those things to me
   if none of it were true.
And why you would bring me that day
   so very close to you.

For you didn't have to say
   it was a possibility.
If you knew when you spoke it
   that it could never be.

But that is not what took place
   between us on that day.
And we both know that those were not
   the words you had to say.

When it was time for me to go,
   for me to be on my way.
You drew me close, one more time
   as if begging me to stay.

So once again we stood there,
   you and me, face to face.
And I felt as if I had been taken
   to an enchanted place.

In a place where I heard music
   and I heard the angel's sigh.
We were there together
   in that magic, you and I.

But this time I really had to go
   yet you lingered one more time.
Then you brought me back so close to you
   and our fingertips entwined.

Yet it was just a simple cup of coffee.
   "I'd like that," is what you said.
How could all this have happened
   and how could I have been misled?

There's a danger in trusting
  somebody too much
A danger in getting so close
  they can touch.

For they enter into a place
  so sacred to you
And they treat you as if
  everything were true.

Then one day you find
  your heart is stripped bare
And it leaves you screaming
  in pain and despair.

Yes, there's a danger in trusting
  somebody too much
And letting them come so close
  they can touch.

For you must protect
  your heart so naïve
From those whom you trust
  but who easily deceive.

You didn't say you were sorry
   you didn't make amends
   you didn't try to heal the hurt
   or to help this heart to mend.

You told me things you didn't mean
   you did some things as well
   and then when my heart believed
   it was then that it fell.

It fell into that bottomless pit
   where broken hearts descend
   where the pain and tears consume
   and the darkness never ends.

So please, I ask you one more time
   to help take away the pain
   to dry the tears and heal the hurt
   and help me to live again.

Gentle hearts can become fractured hearts,
   they trust when others do not;
   they see what others do not see;
   they go where others fear to go.

And in doing so, they open themselves to danger.

For gentle hearts are innocent hearts,
   and are easily taken advantage of
   and broken beyond repair.

I watch the graceful butterfly as it alights atop the petaled flower.
Its colors so vibrant in the bright sunshine.
It visits flower after flower, drinking in the sweetness they have to offer.

I once felt like that butterfly, as my heart was lifted gracefully and I was given colorful wings that carried me and I drank in the sweet nectar of your words.

But the summer flowers soon fade and harsh winds sometimes blow, and some flowers, like cruel words can sometimes poison and kill.

And the graceful butterfly flies no more.

Do you know that you sang to me
  a song so sweet;
And all I wanted was to be near you
  and to have you near to me.

For you made my heart tranquil
  and it danced and came alive;
But the song abruptly ended
  and that day my heart died.

Sometimes I become very angry
   at what you stole from me.
Like a thief you came in and
   took something that wasn't yours to take.
You stole my trust…
   you took that away from me.
You stole my innocence…
   an innocence that I was regaining for myself once
     again.
You stole my heart…
   a heart so fragile and afraid.
And I become angry because you came in
   and you took these things from me
   and then you decided that you didn't want them.

But then I stop because I have to think
   that maybe it wasn't entirely you…
   because I gave you my trust;
   and I gave you my innocence;
   and I gave you my heart.

So if I gave them to you
   did you really steal them from me?
I gave them willingly because that is
   what I thought you wanted,
   that is what your words said.

So if I gave them to you,
   I guess I cannot blame you for stealing them,
     can I?

Michele Spaccarotella

If you didn't want to get involved
  why did you even start?
Why did you do the things you did
  that awakened my hurting heart?

And why did you continue
  if you knew that I believed?
Because you didn't want to get involved
  yet you so easily deceived.

So I heard the words you told me
  but you never did explain.
You ran from me, you broke my heart
  and left me with all this pain.

You didn't say you were sorry
 no need to apologize.
You didn't take the time to see
 the tears that were in my eyes.

You took advantage of my innocence
 and my very vulnerable heart.
You walked right in, left open the door
 and my world just fell apart.

So you boldly took that risk,
 you threw caution to the wind.
And the things you said and did
 you would later rescind.

They weren't true, you told me
 you didn't mean a thing.
I guess it was just a game for you
 and I was just a fling.

Michele Spaccarotella

I was a fool to believe you,
  to hope what you said was true;
  to think that there could ever be
  something between me and you.

I was a fool to dream,
  to let my heart come alive;
  for things are not always what they seem
  and hopes can shatter and die.

I was a fool to let you touch me,
  to touch me like you did;
  to let you take my hand
  and to follow when you bid.

You took my hand in yours
  and you led me in this charade
  and I took down the walls
  because with you I wasn't afraid.

You watched as I started falling
  and maybe you were even amused;
  but when I asked you to explain
  you walked away, you had refused.

For I let your words woo me
  and I let all you did entice
  and in the end, when all was done
  it was my heart that had paid the price.

For in this game you played with me,
　　this game where you made the rules;
　　you were the winner and you walked away
　　and I was made the fool.

I've shared so much of who I am
  and it is easy to see;
  there really isn't all that much
  for you to learn about me.

I don't have that much to give
  but what I have is yours;
  I'm simple and quiet and don't seek much
  but truth and caring and a gentle touch.

There was a time when you sought me out,
  to get to know what I was about;
  but then you ran so far away
  and you gave no reason why you wouldn't stay.

So if you're looking for these things,
  for a heart that's gentle and true,
  then I'm still here, I haven't gone
  I'm still waiting for you.

You had no right to tell me
  things you didn't mean
  or to hold my hand so snug in yours
  or to give your shoulder on which to lean.

You had no right to touch me
  a touch that suggested more
  or to come so close that you were able
  to open up that door.

You had no right to give me
  the hopes you gave my heart
  or to offer me no reasons
  when you later chose to depart.

You had no right to take advantage
  with the cancer by my side
  knowing that I was alone
  and how it terrified.

You had no right to break me
  to make me cry and grieve,
  for my crime was a crime of innocence
  and all I did was believe.

The tears still come, the heart still cries
  the pain hasn't gone away
  it cannot heal the hurt inside
  because of all you wouldn't say.

Michele Spaccarotella

But I know one thing and that is this
  I did nothing wrong to you,
  all I did was to trust
  and then found out it wasn't true.

If one chooses not to see,
does that make that which they
do not see, nonexistent…
and perhaps never was?

The unknown hurts more than the known.
It leaves open the door to the "why?",
    the "how come?", the "what is wrong with me?".
The unknown invites in those voices that ask
    "what did I do wrong?".
The demons haunt and they tease because the
    unknown gives no answers.
And even if what is known may be painful,
    what is unknown can kill.

You can still be that hero
   the one I've been waiting for
   the one who came into my life
   and made my hurting heart soar.

You can still take away this pain
   if you reach inside your heart
   and gather all your strength and courage
   and be willing to make a new start.

Set aside the fear you have
   and be willing to look inside
   let the kindness and compassion
   overtake this foolish pride.

A pride that thinks there is no need
   to comfort or explain
   who thinks it simply is O.K.
   to avoid the one in pain.

So please be willing to try once more
   pray for the courage you hold
   and come to me once again
   and leave behind that heart turned cold.

Do not be afraid to tell me why
   you ran from me like you did
   or why the heart I saw in you,
   you took away and hid.

There is a wealth of good in you
   that lies within your soul
   be willing to help ease this pain
   and give back the heart you stole.

For you entered into a private place
   and woke my heart from its sleep
   and brought it so close to you
   then decided not to keep.

So be the hero I thought you were
   reach down deep within your soul
   have the courage to give back to me
   the heart you don't want, the one you stole.

I HAVE

Have you ever had your heart broken by someone you cared about and trusted?
Have you ever felt the pain so deep as fragments broke, falling and dying?

Well I have.

Have you ever cried yourself to sleep at night as the pain consumes, feeling deep sadness and wondering if it will ever end?
Have you ever cried tears, so many tears, tears enough to fill an ocean?

Well I have.

Have you ever been afraid to trust again, fearing the hurt and rejection, fearing its return and then finding, without looking, someone who you wanted to open up to?
Have you ever taken that step, believing and then letting go of the fear because you know there is gentleness and goodness within the heart of another?

Well I have.

Have you ever been given a reason to look forward to tomorrow, a reason for being, a reason to go on?

Have you ever been made to feel so special, that someone really cared for you and wanted to be with you?

Well I have.

Have you ever heard words so cruel, so hurtful, words that said all the things that you believed weren't true?
Have you ever been so confused, not understanding why and not been given any reasons?

Well I have.

Have you ever been avoided, been run away from and refused to be spoken to?
Have you ever been made to feel so inferior, so worthless, so insignificant?

Well I have.

Have you ever reached out in sadness to right what was wrong and been rejected?
Have you ever hoped and prayed for another chance, a chance to reconcile and to heal?

Well I have.

I hope you never have to feel this pain, for it's a pain that kills hearts.
I hope you never have to hear words that are untrue, words that kill your spirit.

Michele Spaccarotella

I hope you are never avoided by another and feel your
dignity taken away.
I hope you never have to say the words...

Well I have.

If I were a bird
  I'd fly away
  past the moon, the sun, the stars.

Beyond the blackness,
  into obscurity
  until my wings could fly no more.

And maybe in that darkness
  in that far, far distant place
  your memory would vanish
  and I would not still see your face.

For I see your face before me
  when I close my eyes at night
  and I feel your hand that gently held
  and made my heart take flight.

So to fly away would surely be
  the means to set me free
  but I'm afraid your memory won't leave
  it will continue to stay with me.

Michele Spaccarotella

When you're out and about enjoying your life
   and all that your power can bring
   do you ever look back, do you ever see,
   do you ever feel anything?

Do you ever feel the pain I have
   and is there ever any regret
   or was it when you walked away
   that I was so easy to forget?

Or is this the way the game is played
   with another's spirit and heart,
   you fool around, you lead one on
   and then you simply depart?

And why are you afraid to look at me,
   to look into my eyes,
   is it because of what you said
   and all the many lies?

Or do you think that I don't need
   to be given that much respect
   and the wrongs that were done and the hurt I feel
   you have no need to ever correct?

But maybe when your day is done
   and you lay your head to sleep,
   you'll see my face or feel a touch
   and you'll feel in your heart so deep.

For power cannot heal the hurts
   or touch the heart that weeps,
   but love and gentleness can heal all things
   for what you sow, you shall also reap.

Michele Spaccarotella

In the quiet, hearts can hear what the noise
   and the busyness of the world prevents
   them from hearing.
In the quiet, hearts sometimes hear what they do not
   want to hear, so we don't let them become quiet.
It is too painful.

But sometimes, they can hear what another
   heart is saying...
      speaking sweetly...
      speaking directly to them.

Shhhh...listen. Can you hear it?
Listen to my heart.
It was calling to you.

Did you hear what it was saying?
Is that why you ran?

I saw the way you looked at me,
   the way your gaze penetrated me
   past the veil of secrecy.
Why did you do that to me?

If I could run to the edge of nowhere
   and let the vast nothingness
   swallow me and become one with it,
   would the pain cease to exist?

Would your memory cease as well
   and would the pain that never goes away,
   not hurt anymore?

Michele Spaccarotella

THE OLIVE BRANCH

I extend to you the olive branch
   and I ask your forgiveness, please
   for all the hurt, for all the pain
   that has brought me to my knees.

I didn't mean to hurt you
   by what you heard me say
   I had hoped that you would take
   all this hurt away.

Whatever it was that happened
   I ask your forgiveness, please
   and every night, before I sleep
   I get down on my knees.

And I say a little prayer for you
   and a little prayer for me
   that God in heaven will hear it
   and He will let this be.

That He will grant a time for us
   to say what we need to say
   to look each other in the eye
   and maybe find a way.

To let the past be buried
   and start a brand new day
   to forgive the hurt and the pain
   that never goes away.

So please accept this olive branch
  this offering of peace
  and let bygones be bygones
  and the tension between us cease.

That tears will dry and hearts will heal
  and maybe a friendship mend
  for life is too short, too precious
  to let it all come to an end.

The Journey's End...

We have reached the end of the book, but not the end of the journey, for life's journeys do not end until life itself ends. The journey changes, a new one begins. This new journey is called forgiveness and it too is a difficult one. It is the call, the challenge that guides my way. It is the voice of God calling me to follow His way, that of mercy, love and forgiveness. If I claim to hear the voice of God in my life then I must heed His call now to forgive and I find this at times to be most difficult.

Time has passed since I first wrote, but the pain has not diminished. Sometimes I believe that pain to be worse now. Yet despite the pain, I am now called to forgive. I struggle with this daily, knowing that I must forgive in order to heal.

Cancer changes lives and mine has definitely been changed because of this. I have healed well physically and know in my heart that God healed for His work to be done in me. The healing of my heart is a much tougher battle, but not an impossible one. It is one which I must make the choice to do.

Forgiveness is that choice. It is not a feeling, it is a decision that one makes and because it is a decision the emotions are not always in agreement. Yet God calls me to forgive just as I am called to love, for to not do so hinders the love that I am able to give.

Forgiveness does not mean what occurred is acceptable. It does not mean that I do not deserve to be respected. Likewise, it does not mean that I should forget what took place. What it does mean is that I must let go of my hurt and pain, my resentment, my anger, all the worthless feelings and allow God to enter in and let Him reign so that what is almost humanly impossible will become possible with Him. It is in the surrendering of these feelings to Him that I may be set free.

I believe that when one loves deeply, one can be hurt even more deeply. A heart opened wide is left exposed to pain and suffering. But that same heart opened wide to love never loses those we take in. They become a part of us, even though they may reject and leave. They will always remain close. If we do not forgive we hinder that love we have for them.

The anguish, pain, and humiliation that I suffered does not just go away when I say the words that I forgive. It remains in spite of and it is a process that takes time. What happened to me was wrong and I didn't deserve to be treated the way that I was. Despite this, I know that I must make an effort to rid myself of these feelings. It was my hope that I would be given the answers my wounded heart sought. My attempts were fruitless. This makes the journey much more challenging for me. I must let go of my desire to know, relinquishing this to God who understands and allow Him to help me heal. But saying these words does not make it any easier and once again I find where my humanness takes over and like most, I do not do that which I know I must and therein lies the struggle.

By letting go, I allow that decision to forgive to one day become a feeling as well. But it must start with the decision to do so. When I can do this, then I have learned the truth behind the power of love because love and forgiveness go hand in hand. Scripture tells us that love is the greatest gift and it never fails. It is because of love that one can forgive and because God commands us to love one another, we must also forgive one another. I am called now to let God do what I cannot.

It is to Him that I call out. It is to Him I pray that He will help me on this new path and by doing so I will move a little beyond my humanity to reach for a piece of that divinity we all have a part of. With this in mind I write the following and hope it will be received by the one to whom I write it.

I know deep within my heart that you did not mean to hurt me but sometimes we do things we find so difficult to undo. Perhaps that is what happened. Maybe I did something to hurt you as well.

Sometimes it is difficult to see the good in the bad. It is hard to see the blessings when one is in the dark or when one is in pain. It is difficult to see the joy in the middle of sorrow.

You brought to me many blessings when you were by my side. I know that if I wasn't given such joy and happiness then I would not have felt such pain at your leaving.

You gave me hope when I found it difficult to have any.

You gave me strength when I found it difficult to be strong.

In the middle of the cancer you made me feel that you cared and you made me feel beautiful, when all I felt was alone, damaged and so very unattractive.

For a short time you walked with me and that was such a wonderful blessing and one that I will never forget. Our time together was very short, too short, but something that I will always cherish because I know what lies within you.

I want to be able to forgive you and I struggle with this because of the pain that I have. But I want you to know that I am making the decision to forgive. I still pray that you will one day speak to me again, but my forgiveness does not depend on that. If I do not forgive then I lose the gift you were to me. I lose the blessing of you and your memory and the memory of all that was becomes clouded. You and those memories are something that I do not want to lose for memories are so very precious.

I am grateful that God allowed our paths to cross. I would not have chosen otherwise.

I will never forget you. You will remain in my heart. You were my gift, my blessing. Thank you.

Life is a circle.
Our lives intertwine.
Sometimes touching…
sometimes not.

You touched mine.

ABOUT THE AUTHOR

This is the first endeavor at authoring for Michele and one she admits to entering into reluctantly, for opening one's heart is always risky.

Michele has been involved for many years in the charismatic prayer movement. She has been a member of the music ministry in her prayer group as well as a member of a healing ministry. She facilitated a small faith sharing community for many years. She gives of her time at a soup kitchen in her town, believing that she receives far more in return than she gives. Her current ministry is focused on ministering to women, who like herself, are dealing with breast cancer.

Michele resides in the same small town she was born and raised in on the south shore of Long Island, New York. She has two grown children, a daughter and a son.